T0167419

I Can Handle It!

I Can
Handle It!

50 confidence-building stories to empower your child

SUSAN JEFFERS, Ph.D.

bestselling author of *Feel the Fear and Do It Anyway*

and DONNA GRADSTEIN

Jeffers press

Santa Monica, California

A Jeffers Press Book

Copyright © 2002 by Susan Jeffers, Ph.D.
and Donna Gradstein

All rights reserved under International and Pan-American Copyright
Conventions. No part of this publication may be reproduced or
transmitted in any form or by any means, electronic or mechanical,
including photocopying, recording, or any information, storage and
retrieval system, without permission in writing from the publisher.

Published in the United States and Canada
by Jeffers Press, a division of Susan Jeffers, LLC,
P.O. Box 5338, Santa Monica, California 90409

www.jefferspress.com

First published in Great Britain in 2002 by Vermillion,
an imprint of Ebury Press – Random House Publisher's

Cataloging-in-Publication
(Provided by Quality Books, Inc.)

Jeffers, Susan J.
    I can handle it! : 50 confidence-building stories to
empower your child / Susan Jeffers and Donna Gradstein.
-- 1st Jeffers Press ed.
    p. cm.
    SUMMARY: A book for parents, teachers or caregivers
to read with young children. In this collection of brief
stories, children describe in their own words how they
were successful in difficult situations, such as ones
involving fear, frustration, pain, sadness, loss, anger,
embarrassment, responsibility, and guilt.
    Audience: Ages 3-7.
    ISBN-13: 978-0-9777618-0-7
    ISBN-10: 0-9777618-0-0

    1. Self-confidence in children. 2. Emotions in
children. [1. Self-confidence. 2. Emotions.]
I. Gradstein, Donna. II. Title.

BF575.S39J46 2006   158.1
                               QBI06-600170

Printed in the USA
First Jeffers Press edition published 2006

Cover and text design by Dotti Albertine
Original Illustrations by Martin Lovelock
Other Illustrations by JupiterImages

DEDICATION

To parents, teachers, and
all the other everyday heroes
who take care of children
everywhere.

ACKNOWLEDGMENTS

To the children we interviewed who eagerly gave us so many wonderful insights as to which problems they wanted to learn how to handle.

To our own children who, over the years, have taught us both so much about *handling it!* And special thanks to Joscelyn, Donna's seven-year-old daughter, who was always *on-call* to answer our questions about the best way to reach our young audience. She is a jewel.

To Donna's mother, Mildred, for her loving support throughout the writing of our book. We BOTH love and appreciate her so much.

To our husbands, Mark Shelmerdine and Henry Gradstein, who contribute so much joy to our lives. How lucky we are!

To each other ... for having the courage to write a book together given our long-standing and loving friendship. Whew! We handled it!

If you knew
you could handle anything
that came your way,
what would you possibly
have to fear?
The answer is NOTHING!

SJ

C O N T E N T S

SUSAN'S
GUIDE FOR PARENTS

(and Others Who Love
to Empower Children)

I Can Handle It! is a confidence-building book for you to read to and enjoy with your child. And the "you" we refer to here includes parents, teachers, grandparents and all others who take care of children.

I Can Handle It! is based on the affirmation...

> **"Whatever happens to me,**
> **given any situation in my life,**
> **I will be able to handle it."**

This affirmation was first popularized in my book **Feel The Fear And Do It Anyway** and variations of it have been a part of all of my subsequent work. How gratifying it is to now create a book for children that is based on this powerful affirmation!

I Can Handle It! introduces you and your child to 50 children who are learning the "**I can handle it**" lesson. Their stories reflect so much of what is real in the lives of many, if not all, children as they journey through their early years.

What is beautiful is that these stories all have happy endings. That is, the children learn that they can handle whatever life hands them. In this way...

**Each situation, *good or bad,*
becomes a stepping stone for
inner growth.**

I can't think of a happier ending than that!

While the actual stories are fictional, they
were derived from interviews with children who
were very candid as to what truly upsets them.
When asked what concerned them the most,
they were very quick to mention the three
D's...doctors, dentists, and darkness! But there
was so much more.

As the Contents page shows, we divided the
concerns of the children into ten categories:
*Fear, Frustration, Pain, Sadness and Loss, Big, Big
Loss, Anger, Embarrassment, Responsibility, Guilt,*
and dealing with *The World.*

If you think back on your own life, you may
relate to the sentiments in each of the above
categories. We all seem to go through a similar
journey when it comes to developing a sense of
confidence within ourselves. And we continue
on this journey throughout our lives...which is
why adults can learn as much as children when
it comes to the **"I can handle it"** lesson. As you
will discover...

"I can handle it" is a powerful, yet simple, affirmation that can give us all...young and old...a wonderful feeling of confidence and peace of mind.

A word about affirmations: An affirmation, as I am using it here, is a strong, positive statement telling us that "All is well"...despite what the negative chatter in our minds may be telling us. And if we repeat an affirmation to ourselves over and over again, our conscious and subconscious minds begin to believe it is so.

The frequent repetition of an affirmation can eventually quiet that inner "Chatterbox" that makes us feel insecure, frightened, and weak.

It is a very powerful tool to help us push through even the worst of our fears.

You can tell that I am a strong believer in the use of affirmations to help us change our negative thinking and help us feel more powerful and loving in our interactions with the world around us. For example, if I find myself feeling fearful or upset about any situation in my life, I begin repeating an appropriate affirmation over and over again until peace envelopes me like a warm blanket.

A few of my favorite affirmations include...

It's all happening perfectly.
I let go and I trust.
I know that I count and I act as if I do.
I focus on my many blessings.
(And, of course...)
No matter what happens, I can handle it.

I am such a strong believer in the power of affirmations, that I have created a series of affirmation books and tapes[1] and I include a daily affirmation on my website.[2]

Affirmations have long been considered by many to be a valuable tool for adults. I believe that the affirmation can be a valuable tool for children as well. In fact, children probably can learn to use affirmations much more easily than adults. After all, they haven't had as much time

---

1. The "Fear-Less Series" of affirmation books and tapes (*Inner Talk for Peace of Mind, Inner Talk for a Confident Day* and *Inner Talk for a Love That Works*).
2. www.susanjeffers.com

to develop the habit of thinking negatively. And we all know how hard it is to break bad habits!

Also, children love the repetition of simple phrases. The key to positive results with affirmations is repetition, repetition, repetition. And what a great phrase to repeat over and over again...

No matter what happens, I can handle it!
No matter what happens, I can handle it!
No matter what happens, I can handle it!

Why is repetition so necessary? Repetition of a positive thought is necessary to retrain the mind to think in a more positive way. Especially when we live in a world filled with negativity.

Also, affirmations are a form of "acting-as-if". If we act-as-if often enough, our conscious and sub-conscious minds begin to let in the possibility that something is so. And ultimately, we feel *it truly is so*, even though we all need reminders once in a while...even me!

As positive affirmations are repeated over and over again, we become more confident and more loving and our interaction with the outside world subtly changes. Our vast inner resources which allow us to create beautiful lives for ourselves are unleashed. We begin to act differently, stand differently, and react differently. And more often than not, we are treated in a much more positive way by those around us. As you can see...affirmations can be very powerful indeed![3]

Now that you understand the beauty of affirmations, here are some suggestions as to how you and your child can get the most out of this book:

◎ **Read all of the stories on your own before you read them to your child.** If, for any reason, you think a story will be in any way upsetting to your child, then by all means, skip it and go on to the next one. You can always come back to it at another time if you choose. There are so many other stories which your child can learn from and enjoy.

◎ The use of the **"I can handle it"** affirmation, as it appears in this book, teaches children that no matter what happens in their lives, they can handle it all—from spilling juice on the floor, to

---

3. You can learn much more about affirmations and my thoughts about how they are best used in my book, *Feel the Fear...And Beyond.*

losing their favorite toy, to the cruelty of other children, to the loss of a loved one...and much more.

Each of the stories presents just one possibility for dealing with a troubling situation. This offers a wonderful opportunity for discussion. Ask your child questions such as:

"What do you think the child in this story is feeling and why?"

"Do you ever feel the way the child in this story feels?"

"What are some other ways this situation could have been handled?"

"How would YOU handle this situation?"

You get the point. Keep asking questions. You will probably get some very interesting insights about how your child thinks and feels.

By the way, one way to help your child "open up" to his or her feelings is for you to reveal some of your own insecurities as you were growing up. In this way, a deeper sense of closeness and trust can be built between the two of you. Beautiful!

❂ You may not agree with how we portray one of the children "handling" something in a particular story. One of your choices is simply not to read this story to your child. Another alternative is to read it and explain why you don't agree with how the situation was handled. This offers a further opportunity to discuss various other possibilities with your child. Remember that these stories are just idealized examples of the **"I can handle it"** lesson in action. They are models of positive behavior. Certainly, not all children see things or react in the same way. Neither do all adults.

❂ Don't hurry through these stories. They are surprisingly thought-provoking and there are so many wonderful lessons to digest. Allow discussions to naturally unfold. You may find that two or three stories at a time will be enough... sometimes more, sometimes less.

⊚ It is key to remember that each of the stories offers positive suggestions as to how a *specific* difficulty in life can be handled. However...

> **The aim of "I Can Handle It!" is to help your child realize that ALL difficulties in life can be handled in a powerful and loving way.**

You can see why keeping the simple affirmation **"I can handle it"** in the forefront of our minds makes a big difference in the quality of our lives. It certainly beats living with an "I CAN'T handle it" frame of mind!

⊚ Each time you read the affirmation **"I can handle it,"** you may want to have your child repeat it with you. The more often BOTH of you say it, the better BOTH of you will feel in terms of self-empowerment.

◎ As you read, you can point out to your child the words **"I can handle it"** on each of the pages. These words are always in **bold** text. Soon your child may recognize them. Who knows? If he or she isn't reading yet, this may be the beginning of his or her ability to read.

◎ Of course, **I Can Handle It!** can be read to children any time of the day. But, it makes a great bedtime read. Hopefully, the last thing your child will think about before nodding off to sleep is **"No matter what happens, I can handle it."** That's a very powerful message for ALL of us to relax into as we fall asleep at night.

◎ Make **I Can Handle It!** a family affair. Encourage older brothers and sisters to read it to their younger siblings. Grandparents and other adults could also be enlisted as readers. In that way, EVERYONE can benefit from the valuable **"I can handle it"** lesson and develop their own inner resources to deal with the various situations which may arise in their own lives.

❀ I suggest that you put the affirmation **"No matter what happens, I can handle it"** on little notes in your child's room and throughout the rest of the house. Stick them on the refrigerator, on the desk, on some mirrors, or anywhere the affirmation can be seen.

> **Sometimes a little reminder is all that we need to bring us a greater sense of peace.**

And if any family members are troubled about something in their lives, just remind them, "Not to worry...you can handle it!" An entire family empowered in this manner can experience life in a more joyful and peaceful way.

❀ We tried to keep the words "kid-friendly", but if your child doesn't understand the meaning of some of the words, it is an excellent opportunity for a vocabulary lesson.

❀ Have fun with the **"I can handle it"** lesson. Lighten up. Laugh with your child. Encourage your child to understand that we are ALL simply human beings doing the best we can. With each step we take toward developing a greater sense of inner strength and confidence, the better we feel about ourselves and the world around us.

These are just a few suggestions as to how to use this book. Ultimately, YOU are the best judge as to how the "I Can Handle It!" stories can be used most effectively for you and your child.

As you will see, **I Can Handle It!** contains an essential message for everyone...

> **You are never too young or too old to believe in yourself...to know that you can act lovingly and powerfully in any situation that ever confronts you.**

I can't think of a better safety net than that!

And now to the humor and wisdom of the "I Can Handle It" stories...

Enjoy!

50

"I CAN HANDLE IT"
Stories

1

I can handle...
FEAR

MICHAEL

Sometimes I feel scared in my bed at night. I think about monsters and nasty insects and bad people in my room. Even though my parents are right down the hallway, I still get scared. But, **I can handle it...**

There are lots of things I can do to make me feel less scared. I can hug my favorite stuffed animal. His name is Roar the Lion. Or I can ask Mommy to buy me a night-light so I can see better in the dark. Or I can keep a flashlight by my bed. I bet monsters and nasty insects and bad people don't like flashlights shining in their eyes. I know I will figure out what makes me feel better. I just have to use my brain. See, **I can handle it!**

No matter what happens, I can handle it!

LISA

I have to sing with the other kids in our school play. I'm supposed to be a singing tree. I'm SO nervous about standing on the stage and singing in front of a lot of people. What if I forget the words? What if all my leaves fall off? But, **I can handle it...**

I was REALLY nervous before I went on stage. But as soon as we started singing, it was so much fun that I forgot about being nervous! My friends and I giggled when the people in the audience clapped and cheered when we had finished...even if we did forget some of the words. It was great! And only a few of my leaves fell off. Now I can't wait for the next school play. Maybe I'll get the part of the dancing duck. I know I won't be nervous the next time. Well, maybe just a little. See, **I can handle it!**

No matter what happens, I can handle it!

PETER

When Mommy and Daddy take me to the
beach, I'm afraid to go into the ocean.
Even when Daddy holds my hand, the
waves make me fall down and the water
goes into my nose and stings my eyes.
I wish I knew how to swim. But,
I can handle it...

I have an idea. Next time, I'll just put my toes in at the edge of the water where the waves won't get me. And if my toes like the water, then one day maybe my ankles will like it too. Then I'll try my knees, then my belly button, then my shoulders. I don't think my nose and eyes will be ready for a while. But when they are, then I will learn how to swim and play in the waves with Daddy. What great fun! Until then, I can build sand castles with my bucket and spade and play with the other kids. That's fun too. I can't wait until I go to the beach again! See, **I can handle it!**

NO MATTER WHAT HAPPENS, I CAN HANDLE IT!

CHARLOTTE

I don't want to go to school today. I'm worried that my Mommy or Daddy will forget to pick me up. What happens if I get left in school the whole night all by myself? That's a scary thought. But, **I can handle it...**

I'm just being silly. Nobody will leave me in school the whole night all by myself! Somebody ALWAYS picks me up. Sometimes it's Mommy. Sometimes it's Daddy. And if they can't pick me up, I know that Grandpa or a neighbor will come and get me. There will always be someone to take me home from school...until I'm old enough to go home all by myself. See, **I can handle it!**

ANDREW

I saw two cars hit each other today. I heard someone scream and lots of people ran over to help. When I saw an ambulance coming, I knew that someone was hurt. Now I'm afraid our car will be in an accident and we will get hurt too. But, **I can handle it...**

There are things I can do to make us safer in our car. I won't make so much noise. I won't fight with my brother or grab his potato chips out of his hands. And I won't stick my finger in his ear which I like to do because it bothers him and makes him scream. That way, Mommy and Daddy can pay attention to the other cars instead of yelling at us to be quiet. And I will ALWAYS wear my seatbelt. I feel better now that I have a plan. See, **I can handle it!**

- 27 -

ROGER

I was with Mommy in this big, big department store. When she was looking at the sweaters, I walked away. When I turned around, I couldn't see her anywhere. I shouted, "Mommy, Mommy," but she didn't come. I was scared. Maybe I was lost. But, **I can handle it...**

I told a saleslady behind the counter that I lost Mommy. The nice lady told me not to worry. She said she would find Mommy. She picked up a telephone and just like magic, I heard my name all over the store and where Mommy could find me. Soon I saw her running towards me. I was SO happy. I wasn't lost any more. She gave me a big hug, but I knew she was very upset with me. She was even crying a little bit. I promised her I would never walk away from her again. And I NEVER WILL. See, **I can handle it!**

NO MATTER WHAT HAPPENS, I CAN HANDLE IT!

EMILY

Today is my first day of school. I'm scared to go into my classroom. I want to stay outside with Daddy. There are SO many kids in there and I don't know any of them. I worry that no one will like me or talk to me or want to play with me. I want to go home. But, **I can handle it...**

When Daddy left, I decided to be brave and talk to some of the other kids. I said hello to one girl, Joanna, and told her that I was afraid to come to school today. She told me that she was afraid too. You know what? I think that ALL kids are a little scared on their first day of school. I'm glad I said hello to Joanna and the other kids. It made me feel good. And I think that it made them feel good too. Being brave and saying hello can be the best way to make new friends. I bet by the end of the week, I'll have LOTS of new friends. See, **I can handle it!**

ANTHONY

Tonight is my first night sleeping alone. My big brother, Justin, who used to sleep with me, moved into the spare room. Now my room seems so big and empty. It's much too quiet without Justin. I miss the funny noises that he makes when he blows his nose. I miss talking to him when we are in our beds. But most of all, I'm SCARED to sleep alone. But, **I can handle it...**

I woke up in the middle of the night. And guess what? Justin was back in his old bed...right next to me. He told me he thought I might be lonely. But, between you and me, I think he was scared too. We decided that sometimes we can stay with each other at night until we get used to sleeping alone. And then he blew his nose really loudly into a tissue and I laughed a lot. I guess some things never change. See, **I can handle it!**

2

I can handle...
FRUSTRATION

HENRY

I'm angry with my feet! I don't understand why they always decide to grow just when my sneakers get to be soft and cozy. Every time Mommy buys me new shoes, they feel hard and feel strange. But, **I can handle it...**

Sometimes it's hard to get used to something new, but you just have to. I guess growing bigger means wearing bigger sneakers. And I like growing bigger. I bet I will have to get used to a LOT of new shoes before I grow up all the way. It's silly to be angry with my feet for getting bigger. After all, I don't want to be a big, big boy with little-kid feet! See, **I can handle it!**

No matter what happens, I can handle it!

HELEN

I hate getting ready for school. It's too much rushing around. I have to get up, get dressed, brush my teeth, comb my hair, get my backpack ready, and eat my breakfast. I go as fast as I can, but Mommy keeps yelling, "Hurry up, Helen!" Maybe she thinks my real name is "Hurry-Up-Helen". It's not. It's just plain "Helen". But, **I can handle it...**

I know what I can do. I can get my backpack ready and pick out my school clothes BEFORE I go to bed. I'll ask Mommy to wake me up a little earlier. Then I won't be so rushed. I bet I can even get to the breakfast table before Mommy does. Then I can yell, "Hurry up, Mommy!" That would be funny! And then my name will just be "Helen" again...without the "Hurry-Up" part. See, **I can handle it!**

ELIZABETH

I wanted to wear one green sock and one blue sock to school this morning. But Mommy said no. She made me put on two blue socks to match my dress. That's not fair! I don't want to wear two blue socks. I want to wear what I want to wear! I told Mommy, "If you can't wear whatever socks you want, what left in life is there?" But, **I can handle it...**

Mommy said that we should compromise ...whatever that means. We decided that I'll wear two matching socks when I go to school, but in the house, I can wear whatever socks I want. I like that idea. So Mommy picks my school socks and I pick my at-home socks. Now we are BOTH happy. Maybe that's what she meant by "compromise". I'll ask her. See, **I can handle it!**

WAYNE

Daddy took me to the toy shop to buy me something special because I have been a very good boy. I was so excited! I walked all around the shop. There were so many toys I wanted, but Daddy said I could only pick ONE. I just couldn't make up my mind. Finally, Daddy told me that if I didn't hurry up, we would have to leave the shop without buying anything. I felt like crying because sometimes I just don't know what to choose. But, **I can handle it...**

I think I know why it's so hard to choose things sometimes. It's because I don't want to make the WRONG choice. That wouldn't be good. But Daddy told me that there are no wrong choices. I can be happy with whatever I choose because everything has good things about it. Sometimes you just have to look for what they are. So from now on, I won't be upset about making choices. I'll find something good in every choice I make. Do you want to know what toy I FINALLY picked? It was a really cool robot that can pick things up. It's great! See, **I can handle it!**

No matter what happens, I can handle it!

DENISE

I'm BORED! I just came home from school and everybody is busy. My Mom is working on her computer, my sister is doing homework and my Dad isn't home from work yet. Even the dog is sleeping. NO ONE IS PLAYING WITH ME and I've got nothing to do. But, **I can handle it...**

Guess what I did! I went to my room, sat on the floor, closed my eyes and pretended that my room was empty. I imagined that all my toys and games and puzzles were gone. No books, no bed, no chair, no desk. There was nothing at all in my room! Then I opened my eyes and took a good look. My room was FULL of my stuff! All the things that I love to play with were there. There was so much to do! So I started playing ALL BY MYSELF and I wasn't bored any more. See, **I can handle it!**

No matter what happens, I can handle it!

JAKE

Lots of other kids know how to read already, but not me. I try and try and try, but I can't do it. I really want to read like the other kids. I just don't know how. But, **I can handle it...**

My teacher, Mrs. Dickinson, says that we all learn to do different things at different times. She's right! I can already tie my shoes and count to twenty. Some kids can't. It's okay if I can't read yet. I'll just keep practicing and practicing and one day I'll just be able to read. I want to read very, very BIG books when I grow up. I think for now I should just be proud of what I can do, and not worry about what I can't do. See, **I can handle it!**

NO MATTER WHAT HAPPENS, I CAN HANDLE IT!

MARY

Nobody listens to me. I keep trying to talk, but everyone tells me to wait. Wait for what? I have important things to say. I don't like waiting to talk because it's too hard to wait. But, **I can handle it**...

My Mom told me that she is very interested in hearing what I have to say. But sometimes when I want to talk, it's not a very good time... like when she's on the telephone, or when someone else is talking, or when I'm supposed to be listening. Sometimes I need to wait and THEN it will be my turn. The next time I want to say something, I'll just wait my turn and then everyone will listen to me. See, **I can handle it.**

**NO MATTER WHAT HAPPENS,
I CAN HANDLE IT!**

JOE

My older brother, Paul, won't stop teasing me. He pokes me when no one is looking. He calls me a little shrimp all the time. I'm not even sure what a shrimp is, but I know I'm not one. And sometimes at dinner, he puts potatoes and peas with ketchup in his mouth all at the same time...and then he sticks his tongue out at me. That's disgusting! But, **I can handle it...**

My friend told me that his older brother teases him all the time too. I suppose that's just what older brothers do sometimes. They're really weird. I asked my big brother, Paul, when he's going to stop acting so stupid, but he said he wasn't sure. Oh, well. I don't think I can stop Paul from teasing me, so instead of letting him upset me or hurt my feelings, I'll just laugh or not pay any attention to him at all. See, **I can handle it!**

No matter what happens, I can handle it!

3
I can handle...
PAIN

JOSSY

My Mom told me a million times not to
jump on the bed, but I didn't listen to her. I
kept jumping...

> up and down,
> up and down,
> up and down.

Then I fell off the bed and broke my leg.
Wow...did I scream! It hurt more than
anything in the world. Now I have to wear a
cast. It feels tight and it bothers me. I
can't walk fast or swim or play games
outside. I'm just so unhappy. But, **I can
handle it**...

My doctor told me that soon the cast will feel more comfortable and in four weeks he'll take it off. When he does, my leg will be as good as new. I am marking each day on my calendar. Breaking your leg is scary and it hurts for a while. But now I know that broken bones do get fixed and that I have to be a better listener when my Mom tells me not to do something! See, **I can handle it!**

No matter what happens, I can handle it!

JOSE´

My Mommy says today I have to have my teeth checked. I've never been to the dentist before and I'm scared. Maybe the dentist will hurt me. But, **I can handle it**…

Going to the dentist wasn't bad at all.
Dr. Shepard had a fish tank in her office and picture books to look at while we were waiting. When it was my turn, I climbed into this special chair. Dr. Shepard pressed a button and the chair went all the way up and my head went all the way back...kind of like a new ride at the fair. Then she told me to open my mouth VERY wide and she checked every tooth. Even though it was a little uncomfortable to hold my mouth open for so long, it didn't hurt at all. When I was all done, Dr. Shepard gave me a brand new red toothbrush, which is my most favorite color in the whole world. I didn't want to go to the dentist at first, but once I got there, it was really okay. See, **I can handle it!**

**NO MATTER WHAT HAPPENS,
I CAN HANDLE IT!**

ALICE

My friend, Amanda, got a terrible pain in her side. Her doctor told her that she had to go to the hospital to get her appendix taken out. She even had to sleep there for a few nights. I hope I never have to go to a hospital. But, if I do, **I can handle it...**

My Mom took me to visit Amanda in the hospital. I thought she would be very unhappy. But she was sitting up in bed, watching television, and eating chocolate ice cream! My favorite kind! Amanda said her side really hurt at first and she was still a little sore, but now it mostly hurts when she laughs! She will be all better in a little while. Amanda's doctors and nurses took very good care of her and helped her get well. And lots of people visited Amanda. I brought her a Get Well balloon. If I have to have my appendix taken out, I know the doctors and nurses will take good care of me. Maybe I will get chocolate ice cream and lots of balloons too. That's the best part! See, **I can handle it!**

NO MATTER WHAT HAPPENS, I CAN HANDLE IT!

MICHAELA

That's it! I don't want to have any more shots for school. The thought of them just ruins my day! They hurt too much and that's why I don't like them. But Dr. Copeland told me that the medicine in the shots will keep me from getting very, very sick. I don't want any more shots but I don't want to be sick either. What am I going to do? I'm not sure. But, **I can handle it...**

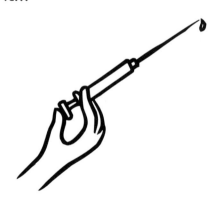

I talked to Dr. Copeland and he told me even though shots do pinch a little, the pain doesn't last long at all. I guess it's not SO bad. Now that I think about it, sometimes I fall and scrape my knees very badly when I'm playing with my friends. That hurts MUCH more than a shot. But that doesn't stop me from playing with my friends. I guess a little pinch shouldn't stop me from having more shots either. I think next time, Dr. Copeland will be very proud of me for not worrying so much about a silly old needle. I'm not going to let the thought of a shot ruin my day any more. See, **I can handle it!**

No matter what happens, I can handle it!

4

I can handle...
SADNESS & LOSS

GARY

I lost my favorite bear. His name was Curly and I've had him a long, long time...ever since I was born. And now he's gone. I looked everywhere for him—under the bed, in my closet, in the yard, and even in the bathroom. But I can't find him anywhere. Maybe Curly is lost forever. I'm sad. But, **I can handle it...**

I'll look again for Curly tomorrow. There are a lot more places he could be. Maybe I'll find him. Maybe I won't. Sometimes bears do get lost, you know! And if I can't find him, I know one day I'll have a new favorite bear. But, I won't ever forget Curly. I'll remember that he was the very first bear I ever loved. One thing is for sure...next time, I'll be much more careful where I put my favorite bear! See, **I can handle it!**

- 65 -

NICK

My tortoise, Jimmy, died. I thought I took really good care of him, but he died anyway. It makes me sad because I miss him so much. But, **I can handle it...**

My Mom told me that even though I did such a good job taking care of Jimmy, he just got sick. She said that these things happen sometimes. I'm sad that Jimmy died, but he lived a long time and had a good life…for a tortoise, anyway. Maybe one day I'll get another turtle, or maybe something else…like a snake! That would be fun. I bet Mom would love to have a snake in our house! I'll ask her while she's making dinner tonight. See, **I can handle it!**

No matter what happens, I can handle it!

LILY

My Dad got a new job and now we have to move to another town. I don't want to move. I will miss my room. I will miss the big tree in front of my house that I love to climb and swing on. And what about my friends? I will miss them too. But, **I can handle it...**

I'm finally getting used to my new house. My bedroom is smaller and there is no climbing tree outside. But there is a beautiful hillside that I can see from my window. My dad says he will take me hiking there. I can't wait. I really missed my friends at first. They missed me too. My teacher from my old school sent me a BIG card with hearts all over it signed by everyone in my class. That made me feel good. And I've already started making new friends here. One girl, whose name is Sophia, makes me laugh a lot. We whisper in class and the teacher always says, "Shhhh." I think I'll ask my mom if Sophia can come over to play tomorrow. If we ever have to move again, I won't feel unhappy. Now I know that no matter where I go, I will make new friends and I will find lots of new things to do. See, **I can handle it!**

NO MATTER WHAT HAPPENS, I CAN HANDLE IT!

JACKIE

My friend, Hillary, had a big fire in her apartment. All her toys were burned in the fire. Even her favorite blue blanket is gone. Now she has to live somewhere else. I don't know what I would do if our house caught on fire and we lost everything too. But, **I can handle it...**

Hillary is living in a different apartment now. My Mom and I went to visit her and we brought her a new blue blanket. When Hillary opened the box, she was so happy. She had a big smile on her face...which looks funny because she's still missing her two front teeth. A lot of people have given clothes and furniture to her family and some new toys to her. Hillary feels good that so many people care about her family and want to help. If we ever have a fire in our house, I think lots of people will help us out and we'll be okay, too. By the way, my favorite blanket is yellow...just in case. See, **I can handle it!**

NO MATTER WHAT HAPPENS,
I CAN HANDLE IT!

GRACE

I feel bad because my big brother, Arthur, is moving far away to go to college. I don't want him to leave. He will be gone a long, long time and maybe he will forget me. I think I will have a missing part in my heart when he leaves. But, **I can handle it...**

Arthur said he loves me and could NEVER forget me. He will miss me too. He promised to write me funny letters while he is away. I know what! I'll draw him lots of pictures to put on his wall so that he will think of me every day until he comes home. I'll still miss being with him, but I won't have a missing part in my heart any more. That's because I know he will always love me no matter how far away he is. See, **I can handle it!**

MADISON

My Daddy is no longer living in our house. He said that sometimes Mommies and Daddies need to live apart. I already knew that because lots of my friends' parents live apart. Daddy says he loves me and always will, and that I will see him often. I'm sad that he doesn't live in our house anymore. But, **I can handle it...**

I get to visit Daddy on weekends and sometimes during the week. We always have such fun together. He reads me lots of books...just like this one. He takes me out for ice cream and he does crazy dances in the street. He makes me laugh so much. I'm so lucky to have such a special Daddy. I know Mommy and Daddy both love me very much and I'm going to be just fine. See, **I can handle it.**

5

I can handle...
BIG, BIG LOSS

RYAN

My friend Bobby's father died. Bobby cried and cried and nothing could cheer him up. He misses his father so much. Now I worry that my father will die too. But, **I can handle it...**

I saw Bobby today. He's still very sad, but he feels a little better. We even played soccer after school. My Uncle Charles told me that when a friend or  someone in your family dies, you always love them and remember them and keep them in your heart forever. If my father died, I know I would miss him just like Bobby misses his father. But I also know that soon I would begin to feel a little better...and my Dad would be in my heart forever just like he is now. See, **I can handle it!**

NO MATTER WHAT HAPPENS, I CAN HANDLE IT!

6

I can handle...
ANGER

EVE

My favorite doll with the beautiful purple dress was a special birthday present from Aunt Evelyn. My friend, Olivia, was playing with my doll. She wasn't being careful and she ripped the beautiful purple dress. I'm very, very angry with her. But, **I can handle it...**

I can't stay angry with Olivia for very long. She's my friend. And I know that Olivia didn't ruin the dress on purpose. It was just an accident. Maybe my mom can sew the dress back together. I hope she can. But it doesn't really matter because I will love my doll anyway, even with a torn dress. And I will still love Olivia too. See, **I can handle it!**

No matter what happens, I can handle it!

JOHN

My little sister, Megan, is ill all the time. My parents always have to take her to doctors, and give her medicine, and spend lots of time with her. They never have enough time for me. So I get very, very upset with them. I even get angry at my little sister, who's only a baby. But, **I can handle it...**

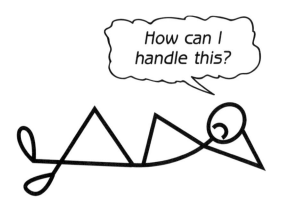

How can I handle this?

It's not my parents' fault that Megan is sick.
It's not Megan's fault either. It's NOBODY'S
fault. I don't even know why I'm angry.
When I think about it, I know I'm lucky. I
don't have to go to doctors all the time and
take medicines that taste horrible. I know
that my parents are very sad that Megan is
so ill. I should be nicer to them and help
them take care of Megan. I could pick up
her toys when she throws them on the
floor. I could sing funny songs to make her
laugh. I could play peek-a-boo with her. She
loves that. And I could be more patient
when she's feeling really bad and my
parents need to be with her. I think if I
helped my parents more, I wouldn't be so
angry. It works like that, you know. See,
I can handle it!

**NO MATTER WHAT HAPPENS,
I CAN HANDLE IT!**

ASHLEY

I used to have my own room, but my new baby brother took it! Why does such a little baby need such a big room? Now I have to share a room with my sister. I don't want to be with my sister all the time. She makes too much noise and won't leave me alone. And she snores. I want my own room back! But, **I can handle it...**

Mommy said that I should look for the good things about sharing a room with my sister. So I looked and looked and looked. And you know what? I found some good things. We get up early in the morning and play together. We talk to each other at night and tell funny stories when the lights are out and we're supposed to be sleeping. And if I get scared at night, she is right there next to me. Now I really like sharing a room with my sister. And I LOVE my new baby brother. See, **I can handle it!**

No matter what happens, I can handle it!

PARKER

One of my friends has a video game player with lots of great games. I want one of those too. My parents can't afford to buy me one. They cost a lot of money. I always have to be invited to my friend's house if I want to play video games. He can play them all the time. That's not fair. But, **I can handle it...**

How can I handle this?

I told my parents that it wasn't fair that I didn't have my own video game player. They said they understood. They said that there are a lot of things that THEY would like to buy for themselves, but they can't afford them either. Mommy needs a new car because hers is very, very old and breaks down a lot. Daddy needs some new suits because his suits are very old. I guess it's not right to be angry at my parents just because they can't buy me everything I want. They both work very hard to have enough money to buy me food and clothes and have a nice place to live. For now, I'll be happy that I have a friend who invites me to play video games at his house. Some day, when I grow up, I'll get a good job and buy anything I want. I'll also buy Mommy a new car and Daddy some new suits. They would really love that...and I would love that too. I think that's fair. Don't you? See, **I can handle it!**

NO MATTER WHAT HAPPENS, I CAN HANDLE IT!

JUDY

In nursery school, we exercise and have to run from this pole to that pole. That's no fun at all. I DON'T want to do it. So today, I wrapped my arms and my legs around one of the poles so I wouldn't have to run. And then I got in trouble. My teacher sent me to the principal's office. That's bad. But, **I can handle it...**

The principal, Mr. Johnson, is very strict.
I know because I've been sent to him
before. Lots of times. This time, he told me
now that I am in school, sometimes
I have to do things I don't want to do. That's
just part of going to school and growing up.
Oh, well. I won't get angry about it any
more. Maybe I will learn to like running
around poles if I keep doing it. Probably not,
but you never know. See, **I can handle it!**

No matter what happens, I can handle it!

7

I can handle...
EMBARRASSMENT

NIKKI

My Mom embarrasses me sometimes. She comes from another country and speaks with a funny accent and her clothes are very different. Some of the kids stare at her when she brings me to school. I just want her to be like all the other Moms. But, **I can handle it...**

How can I handle this?

I have to remember all the reasons I should be very proud of my Mom. She is kind. She sings beautiful songs. She works very hard to give my sister and me nice things. She has a happy face that makes me feel good. I won't care anymore if the other kids stare at her because they don't know how special she is. It's not important what she wears or how she talks. She is my wonderful Mom who loves me with all her heart. I think I'll tell her tonight how much I love her. See, **I can handle it!**

DANNY

Sometimes I wake up in the middle of the night and I have wet my bed. I get upset when that happens. Big kids aren't supposed to wet their beds...that's for babies. It's embarrassing that I even have to tell my Mom. But, **I can handle it...**

I told my Mom how embarrassed I get when I wet my bed. She said there was no reason to be embarrassed because lots of kids my age do that. Then she laughed and said that by the time I go on my first date, I won't be wetting my bed any more. That made me feel better. I wonder when I will go on my first date. I hope it's VERY, VERY soon. See, **I can handle it!**

NO MATTER WHAT HAPPENS, I CAN HANDLE IT!

CARLY

My Aunt has a pretty teacup collection. I was pretending I was serving tea and I broke one of her favorite teacups...the one with the tiny yellow roses on it. When I picked it up, the handle fell right off in my hand. Whoops! I was embarrassed to tell her what happened. But, **I can handle it...**

There is no good way to tell your Aunt that you broke her favorite teacup, except to just say it. When I told her what happened, my Aunt smiled. She said that the handle on that teacup had fallen off fifty times before, and each time she just kept gluing it back on again. I was so relieved. I gave her a big hug and told her she needs to find some stickier glue. We both laughed. See, **I can handle it!**

No matter what happens, I can handle it!

GERRY

I just yelled at Mommy and had a temper
tantrum. I do that sometimes. I threw
myself on the floor and kicked my legs all
around. I screamed as loud as I could. But
Mommy didn't pay any attention to me.
She walked right past me into the other
room. I felt so silly. But, **I can handle it...**

The next time I'm really angry, I'll try not to have a temper tantrum. They look very strange...all that screaming and kicking around on the floor. And if Mommy walks out of the room, there I am, screaming and wiggling around all by myself. What's the point if she's not paying any attention to me? I think when I'm angry, instead of having a temper tantrum, I'll just use a regular voice and tell Mommy what's bothering me. Then she won't leave the room and I won't feel so silly. See, **I can handle it!**

NO MATTER WHAT HAPPENS, I CAN HANDLE IT!

LAURA

I went to a birthday party where we played lots of games. We had a race and even though I ran as fast as I could, I still came in last. Some of the kids made fun of me. They called me "Snail Face" because snails move very slowly. I felt embarrassed. But, **I can handle it...**

My friend, Terry, told the other kids to stop making fun of me. I was happy she stood up for me. That's what good friends do for each other. On the way home, I told Daddy what happened. He said that winning a race is not that important. What matters is that I tried my best. And I really did! Daddy also said there are lots of other things that I CAN do well and that nobody can be great at everything...not even him! If any of the kids make fun of me again, I'll remember what Daddy told me. Then I won't feel so bad. I wonder what "snail faces" look like. I bet they're cute...just like me. See, **I can handle it!**

NO MATTER WHAT HAPPENS, I CAN HANDLE IT!

8

I can handle...
RESPONSIBILITY

JESSICA

When I woke up after nap time at school, my new jacket was gone. It was a birthday present from my Mommy. I think she'll be very angry with me for being so careless. But, **I can handle it!**

I told Mommy that I lost my new jacket but she shouldn't worry...she should just buy me a new one! Mommy didn't like that idea at all. She told me that she would NOT buy me a new one. She told me to look for it when I went back to school, and if I couldn't find it, I would just have to wear my old jacket which is all worn out. Uh-oh. So the next day, I looked everywhere for my jacket. I finally found it in a corner, all rolled up in a ball, just where I had left it. I guess that from now on, I have to be more careful with my things. Mommy isn't going to replace them just because I lose them. They are MY responsibility. And, **I can handle it!**

NO MATTER WHAT HAPPENS,
I CAN HANDLE IT!

G U Y

Today I wrote on the wall with my colored markers. I wrote my name as big as I could.

Guy

Now I can't get it off! Boy, am I in trouble! I know Mom will shout at me because she already told me NEVER to write on the walls. I'm going to be punished....really punished. But, **I can handle it**...

When Mom saw the wall, her face got red and she shouted at me to go to my room and stay there. I have never seen her so angry. When she came into my room, she told me that she would have to paint the whole wall TWICE to cover over the writing. And now she won't let me watch television for two weeks! That's a long time! I guess if you do things you're not supposed to do, you get punished. I don't think I'll write on the walls any more. Then Mom will be happy and I can watch television. See, **I can handle it!**

No matter what happens, I can handle it!

CELESTE

After the rain, I looked outside and saw the big puddles in our garden. I love to jump in puddles so I ran outside and jumped, jumped, jumped all around. It was great fun...until I looked at my new shoes. They were muddy and all wet. I thought they were ruined. But, **I can handle it...**

How can I handle this?

I ran inside and found Mommy. I showed her my shoes and she said, "Oh, Dear. Why didn't you put on your rainboots?" I told her I was so excited about the puddles that I just forgot. She patted me on the head and asked me not to forget the next time because the shoes were new and cost a lot of money. Mommy and I cleaned up the shoes and put them in front of the heater to dry. We put my rainboots by the door. That way I won't forget to put them on the next time I go outside to jump in puddles. I just love big puddles. See, **I can handle it!**

NO MATTER WHAT HAPPENS,
I CAN HANDLE IT!

MORGAN

Uh Oh! I just spilled some orange juice on the floor! Mommy will be really mad because she just finished mopping the floor. I suppose I wasn't being careful. I hope Mommy doesn't yell at me. But, **I can handle it...**

I'll get a napkin and wipe it all up. It was just an accident. But next time I am drinking my orange juice, I will try to be more careful. I don't think Mommy will be too mad at me because everyone spills things sometimes. And I think she will be very proud of me for trying to clean it up all by myself instead of calling for her to come and clean it up for me. I'm getting to be a really big boy! See, **I can handle it!**

KEN

I begged my parents for a dog. They said no because having a dog was too much work. I promised I would take care of it. Finally, they said okay. We went to the dog pound and adopted Plato, who was so happy to get a new home. I love Plato, even though sometimes I get tired of taking care of him. But, **I can handle it...**

Having a dog really IS hard work. But Plato is my responsibility and I made a promise to my parents to take care of him. And everybody has to keep their promises. So even when I'm tired, I feed Plato and play with him because that is my job. And when I don't feel like taking care of Plato, I think about how much I would miss him if I didn't have him. I would miss the way one ear sticks up all funny when he is listening to me and how he snuggles down on my lap when I'm watching television. I think taking care of Plato is the best job I could ever have. See, **I can handle it!**

9
I can handle...
GUILT

MADELINE

I was playing on the stairs with my friend, Amy, and I decided to see how far I could jump. So I jumped. But I didn't look where I was going and I knocked Amy down to the ground. Her hand was scratched and started bleeding. She was crying and she was angry with me. I felt awful. But, **I can handle it...**

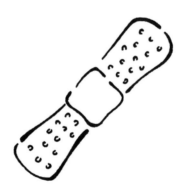

Our babysitter, Katie, washed Amy's hand and put a bandage on the cut. I told Amy that I was so sorry I knocked her down. It was my fault because I wasn't being careful. I didn't mean to hurt her. Then she wasn't angry any more. We decided to do a puzzle together. That was much better than playing on the stairs...and safer too. See, **I can handle it!**

ALEX

Yesterday I took a chocolate bar from the store when my Mommy and the man behind the counter weren't looking. It tasted good, but now I feel bad that I took it. I know it was wrong. But, **I can handle it...**

How can I handle this?

I told Mommy what happened. She was very upset with me. And I cried. She told me that we would have to go back to the store and I would have to tell the man that I took the chocolate. Then I would have to give him all the money I was saving for a new truck. So we went back to the store and that's what I did. The man said that it was very wrong to take something without paying for it, but he was happy that I came back and told him the truth. I was happy I told the truth too...even though I will have to wait a little longer to buy my new truck. See, **I can handle it!**

JON

My Aunt Clara came over for a visit. She asked me how I liked school but I pretended that I didn't hear her and began to walk away. She looked upset. Aunt Clara is a very nice lady. I don't know why I was rude to her. But I was...and I felt really bad about it. But, **I can handle it...**

How can I handle this?

When Aunt Clara asked me why I had walked away from her, I didn't have a good answer. I told her I was sorry and I would try not to do it again. She said that she forgave me. Then she grabbed me and gave me a big, big hug. I could hardly breathe! I'd better not be rude to Aunt Clara any more. If I have to apologize to her one more time, she might not only give me a big, big hug, she might also try to give me a big, big wet kiss! I don't like wet kisses. Yuck! See, **I can handle it!**

NO MATTER WHAT HAPPENS,
I CAN HANDLE IT!

ZOE

I told Libby that she was ugly. She's not really ugly. I was just in a bad mood. She started to cry and ran away from me. I know I hurt her feelings. I feel bad that I was so mean to Libby. I don't like it when kids are mean to me. But, **I can handle it...**

When I got home from school, I told Mommy what happened and that I felt bad. She said, "That makes sense. When you make someone else feel bad, you feel bad too." She said that's called "feeling guilty". Mommy said that if I called Libby and apologized, I would feel better. So I did. I told Libby I was sorry and that I don't really think she's ugly. That made her feel much, much better. And Mommy was right...it made me feel better too. Mommy also said that next time, before I say anything to anyone, I should think about how it will make the other person feel. Boy, sometimes Mommies are SO clever! See, **I can handle it!**

No matter what happens, I can handle it!

FIONA

Granny wants me to sleep at her house tonight and I don't want to. There are creaky noises in the ceiling. And there's a big round clock on the dresser that goes...

tick-tock
tick-tock
tick-tock
tick-tock

The tick-tock clock keeps me awake for hours and hours and hours. I know if I tell Granny that I don't want to sleep at her house, I will hurt her feelings. That will make me feel really bad. But, **I can handle it...**

When I got to Granny's house, I decided to tell her my problems. She was happy I did. First we decided what to do about the creaky noises. We would leave my door and her door open all night, so if I heard a noise, I could call her and she would come running. Or I could sleep with her in her big poster bed sometimes. I would like that. Then we listened to the clock. Granny laughed and agreed that the tick-tock clock is VERY loud, indeed. So we found the perfect place for it in the living room. It won't bother anyone in there, except my Uncle Thomas, who likes to take a nap on the sofa in the afternoon. I'm so happy I told Granny my problems. She fixed everything. Now I won't have to hurt her feelings because I really DO want to sleep at her house. See, **I can handle it!**

NO MATTER WHAT HAPPENS, I CAN HANDLE IT!

10

I can handle...
THE WORLD!

MARK

I was at the airport and I saw a man in a wheelchair. I wondered what happened to his legs. I wondered how he can be happy. People in wheelchairs can't walk and other people have to help them all the time. I feel sad when I see someone in a wheelchair. But, **I can handle it...**

I decided I would go over and say hello. Dad said it would be okay. The man's name was Nigel and he told me he was very happy that I came over to talk to him. He said that lots of children are afraid to talk to people in wheelchairs. That's silly. I'm not afraid! I asked Nigel what happened to his legs. He said that he was in an accident and could never walk again, but most of the time he was very happy anyway. He said that he could do many things by himself. And there are always people to help him with everything else. When people help him, it reminds him how much love there is in the world. I'm glad I came over to talk to Nigel. I think that's a way to show love too. When I had to leave, he told me not to feel sorry for him because every day brings something wonderful into his life...like me! See, **I can handle it!**

NO MATTER WHAT HAPPENS, I CAN HANDLE IT!

LESLIE

I saw a homeless man without shoes looking in a garbage can. I asked my Mommy what he was looking for. She said he was probably looking for old clothes and maybe some food because he didn't have any money to buy anything. That's so sad! Mommy gave him some money. He smiled and said thank you. Mommy said that there are lots of people, even little children, who don't have food to eat and clothes to wear. I wish I could help them. I don't know what I can do. I'm just a little kid. But, **I can handle it...**

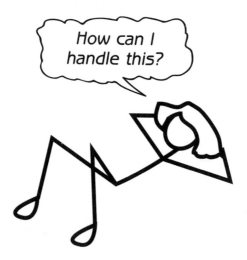

When we came home, I thought and thought and thought about what I can do to help poor people. And I came up with some very good ideas. When my clothes don't fit me anymore because I'm getting so big, I can give them away to children who need them. And I have so many toys and stuffed animals on my shelves. I can give some of them away too. I could even give part of my birthday money to a shelter for people who don't have homes. I talked this over with Mommy, and she thought my ideas were great! So we're going to pack up a whole box of my old clothes and toys and bring them to children who need them. I feel happy now. Even though sometimes it's hard to give your things away, it feels good to help other people. See, **I can handle it!**

NO MATTER WHAT HAPPENS, I CAN HANDLE IT!

STEWART

I was watching television and I saw soldiers fighting each other with guns. It makes me sad to see people fighting. I thought people are supposed to love each other. Why would people want to hurt each other? My Dad says the soldiers are fighting in a war. I don't understand why wars happen. I just don't understand it at all. But, **I can handle it...**

Maybe there isn't enough love in the world and that's why people fight with each other. Maybe I don't act loving some of the time. In fact, a lot of the time! When I am being mean to my sister, I am not being loving. When I am fighting with my brother, I am not being loving. When I want more Christmas presents than everyone else, I am not being loving. When I say, "I hate you" to someone, I am not being loving. Maybe I have to start being more loving. If EVERYONE acted more loving, maybe there wouldn't be any more wars. You know what? I think everyone's love counts. Even mine ...and yours! See...**WE CAN HANDLE IT!**

AUTHOR BIOS

SUSAN JEFFERS, PH.D. is the international bestselling author of many books including *FEEL THE FEAR AND DO IT ANYWAY, END THE STRUGGLE AND DANCE WITH LIFE, EMBRACING UNCERTAINTY, THE LITTLE BOOK OF CONFIDENCE, THE LITTLE BOOK OF PEACE OF MIND, LIFE IS HUGE!* and *THE FEEL THE FEAR GUIDE TO LASTING LOVE.* She has helped millions of people throughout the world overcome their fears, heal their relationships and move forward in life with confidence and love. Dr. Jeffers is also a popular speaker and media personality. Her two children, Gerry and Leslie, and two step-children, Alice and Guy, are all grown up and she lives with her husband, Mark Shelmerdine, in Los Angeles, CA. Her website address is: www.susanjeffers.com.

DONNA GRADSTEIN, J.D. is a founding member of the Los Angeles law firm Gradstein & Luskin. Prior to establishing this law firm with her husband, Henry Gradstein, she was a lawyer for Columbia Pictures and an independent documentary filmmaker. She has five children and lives with her family in Santa Barbara, CA.

By Susan Jeffers, Ph.D. (in alphabetical order)

Dare to Connect: Reaching Out in Romance, Friendship and the Workplace*

Embracing Uncertainty: Breakthrough Methods for Achieving Peace of Mind When Facing the Unknown*

End the Struggle and Dance with Life: How to Build Yourself Up When the World Gets You Down*

The Fear-Less Series

Inner Talk for a Confident Day*
Inner Talk for a Love that Works*
Inner Talk for Peace of Mind*

The Feel the Fear Series

Feel the Fear ... and Beyond: Mastering the Techniques for Doing It Anyway*

Feel the Fear and Do It Anyway: Dynamic Techniques for Turning Fear, Indecision, and Anger into Power, Action, and Love*

The Feel the Fear Guide to Lasting Love*

Feel the Fear Power Planner: 90 Days to a Fuller Life

I Can Handle It!: Fifty Confidence-building Stories to Empower Your Child (for children aged 3 -7) co-authored with Donna Gradstein

I'm Okay ... You're a Brat: Setting the Priorities Straight and Freeing You from the Guilt and Mad Myths of Parenthood*

Life is Huge!: Laughing, Loving and Learning from it All

Losing a Love and Finding a Life: Healing the Pain of a Broken Relationship

Opening Our Hearts to Men: Taking Charge of Our Lives and Creating a Love That Works*

The Little Book of Confidence

The Little Book of Peace of Mind

Thoughts of Power and Love* (quotes from the works of Susan Jeffers)

*Also available in audiotape and/or CD

Audio Tapes from Live Appearances

The Art of Fearbusting (also available in CD)
A Fearbusting Workshop
Flirting from the Heart
Opening Our Hearts to Each Other

www.susanjeffers.com

www.jefferspress.com